The Secret Teachings of the Qabbalah

By

MANLY P. HALL

FIFTH EDITION

Martino Publishing
Mansfield Centre, CT
2013

Martino Publishing
P.O. Box 373,
Mansfield Centre, CT 06250 USA

ISBN 978-1-61427-442-1

© *2013 Martino Publishing*

Cover design by T. Matarazzo

Printed in the United States of America On 100% Acid-Free Paper

The Sacred Magic of the Qabbalah

By

MANLY P. HALL

FIFTH EDITION

PHILOSOPHICAL RESEARCH SOCIETY
3341 Griffith Park Blvd., Los Angeles, California.

The Sacred Magic of the Qabbalah

THE SCIENCE OF THE DIVINE NAMES

INTRODUCTION

The religious teachings of all nations may be divided into two general divisions. The first is the religion of the common people, and is the exoteric faith. The second is the religion of the wise and initiated few. This is the esoteric faith, and seldom, if ever, appears in the world without the cloak of ritual and symbol to conceal it from the uninitiated. The esoteric faith occupies the same position with respect to religion that the spirit holds in relation to its bodies. The bodies bear witness of the spirit. Through the spirit comes the life which animates and vitalizes the bodies. These bodies are often referred to as Matthew, Mark, Luke, and John, the witnesses or recorders of the life of the spirit. Man's four bodies are the evangelists who go forth bearing accurate witness to the spiritual life that animates and gives power to them. In a similar way, the body religious bears witness to the life spiritual. The world recognizes only the body, while the wise and initiated few study only the spirit.

All concrete or visible things belong to the world of effects. These are studied by the esoteric student only that he may discover through them their invisible Cause. True esoterists follow the Aristotelian method of reasoning, using the visible only as a means whereby to know the invisible, studying the multiplicity of effects to become mentally and spiritually aware of the unity lying behind the diversity in Nature.

Behind the veil which conceals the great Unknown stretches the world of causation, the invisible side of Nature. It is not given to man at the present time to understand the mysteries of this prototypal sphere. The veil of *Maya* which divides the world of men from its source, the world of God, is not really a structure or fabric but rather the line of limitation. The things that lie beyond the hypothetical circle which surrounds man are unknown because they are too attenuated and subtle to be recorded by the senses thus far developed by the human race.

This invisible world is explored only by a few hardy travelers who, striking out from the human race, brave all in their efforts to chart and map the great vistas of eternity. These daring ones are rewarded for their efforts by being accepted into the Invisible. They become citizens of two worlds, and are known as the Initiates and Masters. Only those who have gradually learned the subtle laws of the invisible Nature are permitted to pass beyond the veil.

All the arts, philosophies, and sciences which surround us in the material world are effects and doctrines concerning effects; for when they have become concrete or organized, and have reached that point where they can be grasped by the human mind, they have come across from the intangible to the tangible and have assumed, to a partial degree at least, the veil of substance. They have taken on coats of skins, and in becoming one with men have severed their connection with the Infinite. As the body conceals the spirit, so within the soul shrine of every philosophy and religion is hidden a living, divine, glowing coal. This fiery radiance is the esoteric power, or the spirit of every art and science. It is that part of the human being which still preserves its divine element. With the sword of discrimination man must sever the true from the false, the head from the body, the spirit from its sheath of clay.

Philosophy is a concrete, exoteric study, but within itself it conceals occultism, the mystical

[5]

philosophy of the soul. The former bears witness to the latter, for both are one. The visible, tangible body is for the materialist and those who are wedded to form, while the invisible body is for those few who can realize its existence because of special training along the lines of mystical thought. The Craft Mason with his geometry conceals behind his exoteric rituals the geometry of natural law. Beneath chemistry alchemy lies hidden, waiting to give to those who can search its depths the secrets of spiritual transmutation and the chemistry of life. Religion, as we know it, prepares for the path of the mystic, for it is unfolding gradually the ideals of service and brotherhood, which are the basis of true mysticism.

The true student of music can never gain the full inspiration of his art until the attuned keyboard of his being registers the music of the spheres, for these are the eternal harmonies in Nature. No artist has ever really learned color, no lawyer or physician his profession, until its hidden side has been understood, and no student of modern religion can unlock his sacred books without the twofold key of the Qabbalah.

The Bible, as studied today by the average Christian, is a sealed book. There are few who can sense its meaning, for we can see and understand only those things which are already part of our own natures. From the time of

Moses, the Jews preserved by oral tradition certain spiritual laws or mystic principles, which, when applied to the exoteric documents of Scripture, reveal to those able to use them the unseen spiritual wonders of the Invisible. With these keys the student can unlock many of the hidden sections of religious philosophy and unravel the complicated story of the gods. In the following pages will be found a series of concise statements intended to give the student of the invisible path a few principles or foundation stones upon which to build the superstructure of personal experience and first-hand knowledge. By them he may disentangle the thread of existence and, like Alexander, cut the knot the world has tried so long to untie. Life is the Gordian knot, wisdom the sword of quick detachment. According to the ancient views, the veil between the false and true was composed of draperies of knotted cords and tassels. Each of these knots was placed in a peculiar position in relation to others, and he who can read the cipher of these knots can solve the Qabbalistic mysteries of the Jews.

KEYS OF THE SACRED WISDOM

PART I

1. In studying the sacred sciences the first point that the student must understand is that they will give him no powers or opportunities greater than those which he has prepared himself to receive by the life he has lived. The daily life is the test of the student, and until he lives true to the laws of the mystic temple builders he can never gain anything from the study of the Qabbalah, for the esoteric wisdom is not a series of intellectual facts but a living, spiritual thing which can be recognized only by those who live and think in harmony with it.

2. There is only one reward for those who seek spiritual unfoldment or extension of power without first cleansing the body and the soul. The very powers which the student draws to him in his studies will destroy him unless he is robed in the garments of purity. Unto the unpurified, God is a consuming fire; for wherever dross is in the nature His power will burn it away. With the influx of the spiritual power there is a great cataclysm in the body of man; and if he has not prepared it to the best of his ability to receive this light,

[8]

his foolhardiness will precipitate obsession, insanity and death, for broken bodies, nerves, and minds follow in the wake of broken laws.

3. The student of the Mysteries must learn to be patient. He must be prepared to strive for ages without reward, with no more encouragement than the realization of a life work well done. The power of the true mystic and the insight of the Qabbalist are not assumed, but are slowly evolved by years, nay, lives of unselfish service and self-improvement. Nowhere on the White Path are there any exceptions to this rule.

4. The ancient Qabbalistic magic of the philosophers had nothing to do with fortune-telling, divination, or the so-called art of numerology, for such things were said to be of the earth earthy and it was considered a prostitution to make these great spiritual things serve the human side of Nature. Those who study the Qabbalah to find out their lucky days, the length of their lives, their birth paths, and so forth, are failures before they begin. They prove beyond the shadow of a doubt that they are not worthy or prepared to receive the guardianship of the sacred teachings; for man cannot know truth until he realizes the value of it, nor can he be wise while he seeks anything else but wisdom.

5. The study of man can be pursued success-

[9]

fully only by those who have acquired the qualities of reverence and obedience. Each must have one ideal as his guiding star. Each must study principles and not personalities. With simplicity of heart and clarity of mind he must approach the great mystery. When man abuses his privileges or makes no use of his opportunities to understand Nature's law for his being, he brings down upon himself unhappy Karmic reactions.

6. The old Jewish rabbis taught that those who study the Qabbalah play with fire, and the student of today knows that this is true of all esoteric teachings. Wisdom is a two-edged sword. For that reason, the Mystery Schools demand years of purification and preparation, and the student of the Ancient Wisdom must, without hesitation, accept these obligations if he desires illumination.

7. The curiosity-seeker and those searching for thrills can never gain the sacred truth or fathom the secrets of the Qabbalah. The same is true of those who study magic only that they may derive power therefrom with which to take advantage of people less informed. He who searches for wisdom in order to gain temporal power will never secure the true spiritual light. All who follow such a course are disciples of the Black Path.

8. Only students actuated by the highest mo-

tives and purest ideals can hope to gain true knowledge of this great science concerning the secrets of the soul. Not until the seeker after spiritual illumination so lives that he proves by his thoughts and actions his right to receive the celestial knowledge, will the keys of the sacred sciences—the silver key of the old and the golden key of the new Qabbalah—be entrusted to him.

9. Man must cease his efforts to mold the universe according to his own desires and God's laws to temporal ends. He must realize that he is wise who molds himself into the Divine Plan, and, instead of drawing God and wisdom down to himself, rises through the seven heavens like Mohammed ascending to the footstool of divinity.

10. The student must realize that a balanced intellect to hold emotional excesses in check and a harmonized body through which both the mental and emotional natures may find expression are essential to the understanding of a teaching which is harmonious and bal anced. Only those who have been faithful in little things can ever hope to be given the sacred sceptre of divine power which makes them masters over greater things.

11. In the Hebrew alphabet, consisting of twenty-two letters, are the fundamentals of Qabbalistic knowledge. Each of the letters is

[11]

composed of tiny flames joined together in various combinations, the number of flames to each letter ranging from one to four. With the letters of this flaming alphabet the student of the Qabbalah is first concerned, for they are the basis of a great fire-born doctrine.

12. The ancient Jews declared that it was with various combinations of these flaming points that ADM named all things while in

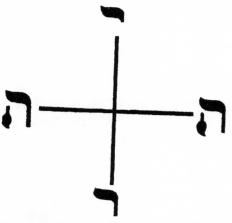

the Garden of the Lord. The student of occult philosophy realizes that everything has both its own true name, which is its eternal word, and also a form or material name which changes with its manifestations. All the true names are based upon various combinations of *Yod,* the great fire flame. *Yod* is the primitive figure or hieroglyph of the Hebrew alphabet. It is the name of the independent fire flames which gather together to form the twenty-two letters. Masons have accepted this symbol as that of God. It is also the first letter of the Hebrew name *Jehovah*.

13. These fire flames represent living forces among the creative hierarchies which we know as the vitalizing or life-giving forces of Nature. Various combinations of these celestial creatures differentiate and vivify all the forms seen in the material world.

14. All differentiation is the result of various combinations of spiritual energies, which cross and recross at different angles according to the receiving poles and centers within the evolving life. The various combinations of these forces in the invisible world spell out the archetypes of bodies, and these bodies become the consonants of the Hebrew alphabet.

15. The vowel points, which were never written by the ancient Jewish people—because they represented divine elements and were too sacred to be symbolized upon paper—represent the life centers which animate and give expression to the consonants or forms. In the same way the whirling vital centers in the human body are the invisible causes which lie behind our visible bodies. As there are seven vital centers, so there are seven vowels; but as two vowels (*w* and *y*) are at the present time only partly used, so certain spiritual centers are

latent under certain conditions at the present time. As no word can be formed without vowels, so no body can be built of consonantal elements alone. Every body must have its unwritten but sounded and admitted life element.

16. The vowel points and their sounds, colors, and forms were grouped together by the ancients as the spirits before the throne, and composed the unspeakable name of the unknowable God. (In the Sanskrit the seven vowels are the *Dhyani Chohans* radiating the life force of Fohat.)

17. According to the Jews there are two great worlds. The higher or superior world was called the *Macrocosm*, and in it rules the divine man, *Macroprosophus*. The lower world or the lesser sphere was called the *Microcosm* (little cosmos), and in it ruled an emanation of *Macroprosophus*, known as *Microprosophus*, or the lesser reflection of the greater. Man made in the image of his Father, the Great Man—Adam Kadmon, the archetype—contained both the nature of the human, or lower, and the nature of the divine, or higher. In order to understand Nature and God, these philosophers taught that man must unravel the mystery of his own being, which was made in the shadow of God, and find the sacred meaning of the twenty-two hieroglyphic letters and

[14]

the vowel points as they play out their drama in the realms of spirit and substance.

18. It is said that there are a number of mysterious forces playing through Nature. These forces are correlated to the letters of the divine name *Tetragrammaton*, which in turn is correlated to the four elements; and these, combined into seventy-two combinations, are referred to as the ministering angels, or the intelligences dwelling in and manipulating the life-giving forces. The celestial language, which we see around us in our world of ever-changing lights and colors, is called the Bible of Nature. The word *Bible* here has its original meaning, *a book*. This book is composed of the consonants of the divine alphabet. When these letters are given meaning and illuminated by the unuttered and unwritten vowel points dwelling within the senses, man then reads his own destiny as it is written by the hand of Divinity.

19. All forms are composed of one substance, the difference being in the combinations and positions of the life centers (the vowels). Nature furnishes the book, but the positions of man's sevenfold consciousness interpret the book. The consonants may, and do, change their meaning through the position of the vowels which give life to their dead forms. The early translators of Jewish literature experi-

enced literally the difficulty that students of the book of Nature experience spiritually. The early Jewish Scriptures were written without vowels and without spacing between words. The confusion which resulted can be appreciated by taking two consonants such as *l* and *g* and trying to reason out whether the word is *log* or *lug* or *leg,* for with the vowel the meaning is changed. It is the same in Nature. The difference between a plant, an animal, and a man, the difference between the intelligences of different men is the result of varying the placing of the vowels (of consciousness) in the consonants (of form).

20. These vowel centers (or life poles) are evolved by the lives we live; and as their position and power are all-important in interpreting the message of life, we lose the faculty of discernment when our lives are out of harmony. The words of life lose their meaning because the vowels are misplaced. In the same way, if we have a certain vowel (center of life or interest) that is over-emphasized, we have a habit of placing it in everything that we see. As a result of this undue emphasis, we distort Nature and become incapable of discrimination.

21. The present relationship of the consonants (bodies) and the vowels (life centers) in man produces a *word* which is not primarily

[16]

a combination of sounds, but rather, like words, is a symbol of an invisible activity; yet in the last analysis it is literally a word. It is the key to the position in the scale of evolution occupied by the life of which it bears witness.

22. Every living thing consists of a sound, a color, and a form; for these are the trinity of manifestations which bear witness to the life within. All colors have a sound and a form; all forms have a color and a sound; and all sounds have a color and a form. The rates of vibration of many sounds our ears are unable to detect. There are numerous colors which we do not see and forms which elude the perceptions of the senses, but nevertheless they exist. Life on every plane of Nature (in the sense of the objective worlds, the Lesser Face) manifests through these three divisions, which are correlated to the powers of the triune divinity.

23. Thousands of years before the radio was discovered Jewish philosophers realized that the world was a checkerboard of criss-crossing, vitalizing currents, alternately positive and negative. This is the checkerboard of the ancient Temple.

24. Man is a human radio, and like this instrument can be attuned satisfactorily to but one rate of vibration at a time. Of the thousands of messages passing through the air

[17]

simultaneously, a well constructed receiving set can be attuned to any one, while all the rest will have no more effect than though they never existed. The more selective the instrument, the higher grade is its mechanism. It is the same with man and the planes of consciousness in Nature through which he is evolving. The scatter-brain, like the cheap instrument, is not sharply selective, and therefore brings in several stations at once. So the finer the receiving equipment, the more perfectly it will receive the spiritual messages of Nature. The differences in our rationality in our natures, and in our spiritual unfoldment are primarily the result of our adjustments with these fire-flaming currents of natural force, function, and intelligence, symbolized by the Jews as the alphabet of Nature, or the elemental letters from which the words of manifestation are formed.

25. Daily and hourly development of body, mind, and spirit attunes us to ever finer currents, whereby we receive an influx of energies from ever higher and finer natural planes. These influxes are the materials with which we are eternally rebuilding our organisms. Consequently the better the quality of the organism, the better the materials it will draw; and the more attenuated and ethereal the source of our vital energies also, the more our

bodies will be molded and attuned with the spiritual spheres of Nature. The more closely our bodies approach perfection in function and organic quality, the more perfect our characters become and the more satisfactory the results of our labors.

26. Everything is created by a word. This word is a rate of vibration, and is said to be the true name of the thing or body which it builds around itself. We may say that bodies are spiritual thoughts put into words. The letters of the alphabet which form the constituents of words in the physical world are the chemical elements. Therefore, our forms are words made up of a certain number of chemicals. An example of this can be studied first hand by the advanced student who sees the word-forms created by the rates of vibration of a person's voice; for man is a creator on a small scale, giving a certain degree of immortality to his though-forms and word-pictures. Hence, he is held responsible by Karma for these invisible creations.

27. The great vibratory fiats of cosmic creation (called in the ancient Qabbalah the *Sacred Names*) when placed in the hands of the wise unlock the mystery of being. In the hands of the foolish, however, they are destructive forces which will ultimately destroy all who seek to desecrate them. They are, in truth, the flam-

[19]

ing letters which illuminate the way of the sincere aspirant, but which burn the unpurified and insincere with a consuming fire.

28. According to the ancient Israelities, the knowledge of the Qabbalah was given by the angels in Paradise to man at the time of his fall, so that he might thereby regain his lost estate. It was perpetuated by Moses and the schools of Samuel the Prophet, during which time it consisted of a series of oral traditions and keys which were communicated solely by word of mouth to those who had proved worthy of the trust. The Qabbalah formed the esoteric teachings of one of the most profound of the Atlantean Mystery Schools.

29. The Qabbalists taught that the body of man consisted of the consonantal letters which on a larger scale formed the body of the Grand Man of the Universe. The vowel letters were the planets—the *Elohim;* and on the walls of the heavens they wrote eternally in ever-changing combinations, concentrating their influence upon the lesser man through the miniature corresponding centers within the human body. (This is undoubtedly the origin of the story of the handwriting on the wall; at least, such are the deductions of James Gaffariel).

30. The vowels, as symbols of the life, were divine; they belonged to God and were His name, for He was considered the composite of

all life energies. In man these are the lotus blossoms or roses that bloom on his cross of matter, and as no word can be formed without a vowel, so no body can be formed without one of these centers. It must be sounded even if not written.

31. Students of the sacred sciences maintain that each nation pronounces its vowels differently. This is due to development of the larynx, for its range and rates of vibration are the results of evolutionary growth. An interesting feature of early Qabbalistic philosophy was that in which the dignity of words was emphasized by the position of the tongue in vocalizing them. Thus in pronouncing the name *God,* it was necessary to raise the tongue to the roof of the mouth as an act of adoration. Again, in speaking the letter *s,* it is necessary to hiss like a snake; for we know that the present form of the letter is derived from the ancient character of a partly coiled serpent. This system was used partly throughout the alphabet and was said to have special Qabbalistic significance. Based upon the formation of the larynx, the Qabbalists taught that every living thing speaks a word, the manner in which it is pronounced denoting the mental, spiritual, and physical status of the body which forms the sound. This is called its true name

[21]

and is the word man forfeits when he loses the ability to know himself.

32. Occult scientists have declared spirit to be air in motion. The ancients also taught that when the rate of vibration which we call matter was raised to a certain point, it became a spark of life. In man this spark is born out of the larynx by the rates of vibration set up by the shape of that organ. This rate of force coming into objectivity, clothes itself with colors, sounds, and forms. Among hashish addicts particularly, it is not an uncommon form of hallucination for them to declare emphatically that while in the state of partial stupor they have seen words coming out of people's mouths. The occultist knows that the use of drugs is one of the easiest methods to secure a negative form of mediumship; for when the conscious mind is thrown into a stupor, certain astral and psychical records are often brought through. Delirium tremens is another familiar example of the same principle. The Ancient Wisdom teaches that man was born out of the mouth of God; for which reason this creative fire that brought him into being by calling him out of the darkness of space is called the Great Name—the keynote of his creation.

33. Let us apply this idea to the problem of everyday existence recognizing that the world

is made up of consonantal elements and that the sense centers evolving within ourselves are the vowel points that bring order and sensibility out of the chaos of confusion and ignorance. The thousands of examples to be seen in Nature and life, when reduced to a composite unit, comprise the Bible or the sacred book of creation. As stated before, however, this sacred book was written without spacing between words and without vowels.

34. To the problems of his existence each individual must apply the keys furnished by his own centers of consciousness. With these Qabbalistic keys of wisdom he must make true logic and sense out of the sacred book, vivifying it with his own life—dividing its letters into words by the powers of discrimination. Only when he has done this can the secret of the Sacred Name be understood, and will he realize that incantation and invocation were merely blinds used by the wise magicians of the ancient world to conceal the true spiritual mystery of ceremonial magic.

35. The Qabbalah can never be written nor can it ever be explained to the profane, for its own depths conceal it. Unrecognized and unknown, it stands behind the veil of human ignorance. The impossibility of materially objectifying this sacred science was well understood by the ancient philosophers. This is the

true reason why there are so few students of the mystic sciences. Like all great things for which man seeks, the student of the Qabbalah must be prepared to pay the price demanded by Nature for the wisdom he receives.

The unwritten law cannot be learned; it must be evolved within the spiritual body of the aspiring seeker through right thought, right emotion and right action. When the student has actually reached the point of self-mastery, then and then only the vowels assume their correct positions; the sacred centers are opened; and the Master's *word*—the key to all creation—is found in man and the student becomes a Master of the Sacred Name.

THE MYSTERY OF THE NUMBERS

PART II

36. According to the Ancient Wisdom, all numbers came forth out of AIN SOPH—the unknown, the dot, the Absolute. The One is the primary manifestation, and as such we are going to consider its power, first in its descent out of the dot and then in its ascent back again into the nature of the dot.

37. Manifesting out of the formless dot, the beginning of all things is a state of one-ness which man calls unity. All things in the world today have one natural origin. All things began as one, which came forth out of No-thing, the Unmanifest, by the "elongation of the dot." To the ancients, *one* indicated the unity of source, and a unified source meant equal opportunities for all. If all things had one source there can be no superiority among them, except that superiority resulting from the victory of action over inaction. In short, we may say that difference is the result of the diligence of some and the indolence of others.

38. Since the family tree of all people can be traced back to the dot—the form of No-thing and the One, its first outbreathing—there is no place in Nature for persons or

things which are superior to or holier than others. All things in unity have equal opportunity and equal possibility. No thing and no one can honestly say that he never had a chance. Either the opportunity was never recognized or, if recognized, the individual did not profit by it or accept the lessons which it sought to teach. Difference in the desire to accomplish and the intelligence of procedure are solely responsible for the inequalities which we see in the world.

39. Within his own soul everyone has the possibility of ultimate perfection and the daily opportunity for relative perfection. These possibilities and opportunities remain dormant, however, until man himself awakens them by aspiration and activity. Perfection—at least, relative perfection—is the undeniable goal of all things, and the length of time we are forced to struggle for it depends largely upon the abilities which we unfold and the application we make of our newborn faculties.

40. Science teaches that all forms are various combinations of one primitive essence. This essence, or *primum hyle,* is the substance of the dot, and manifests through its personification and extension in the One. A stone, a flower, a man, and a god are all stages in the differentiation of one life. A vegetable is in the process of becoming an animal; an animal

is a stage in the unfoldment of a planet; while an electron is a god in the process of becoming. All things are stages in the expression of one connected life, which at the present time is engaged in the task of liberating itself from the dense crystals of physical substance.

41. All thought is a unity; all natural forces which man uses in his various manifestations

are one in their causation. A person's ability to think does not depend upon chance but upon the attuning of his consciousness to the planes of thought, so that his mental powers may be energized. Those who attune themselves to the various planes of Nature governing the major divisions of life will receive the influx of thought, life or power that dwells in and manifests through that particular plane.

[27]

42. The number *one* also governs the reason for man's labor here. There is but one motive in all his works; there is but one end to all his labors. He must seek to unite his intelligence with that of his Creator, the Ancient of Days. This he does by adjusting his organisms to the body centers of the Macrocosmic Man. This sequential adjustment of internal centers of consciousness with eternal qualities we call *evolution*.

The One in its Return to Unity.

43. The one Source of life and the first principle thereof manifests itself in the world as a multiplicity. The one cause, the eternal unit, is diversified into the millions of existing forms, all of which bear witness to the infinite diversity of powers concealed within the structure of the primitive One. Since this unified causation expresses itself as a multiplicity, we recognize it as a stream of ever-evolving individualities pouring out of the abyss of Space through the One and into the Many-ness. This One is like a ray of light which spreads out, to be finally swallowed up in darkness as the spirit is enmeshed in form.

44. All differentiation must be unified without the loss of rational individuality before even a relative state of perfection is attainable. Consciousness in man is always growing. (We

[28]

use the word *growing* to express the idea of spreading out over the area of its bodies.) Its path is from unconscious One-ness to semiconscious Many-ness, and then back again to superconscious unity. When he returns to his source again, however, man has the circle of a completed cycle to add to the extended point of first expression. This is symbolized by the number *ten,* which stands for the completion of the first round, for it is the *one* and the *round,* or cipher. It means that the One has returned to itself after circumscribing the circle of Many-ness.

45. The young soul is a unity of unconscious possibilities; it is One, and yet has in potentiality endless differentiation, for it has not as yet split up its rays through individualization. It is asleep. The old soul, after its wanderings, is again a One-ness, containing within itself the possibilities that it has awakened into dynamic powers; for, having split up its rays to gain experience, it has again united them to a single end. *The young soul is the expression of One pouring itself into Many-ness in search of experience. The old soul has increased its One-ness to contain all diversity and all Many-ness and still remains a unit.*

46. If all things are phases in the unfoldment of one thing and we are seeking to understand that one thing, what is the logical

[29]

course to pursue? Obviously there is but one answer. If its manifestations are reflections of itself, the only way to understand its nature is to master the gamut of its moods. Those who are masters of the complete expression of divine manifestation are masters of the divine will. As long as a single link is missing, man cannot know his Maker. As all things combined in proper proportions form the body of the Grand Man, so all these things combined in the same proportions on a smaller scale produce the transmuted terrestrial Adam, or the symbol of species.

47. All things move and evolve as diversity in unity. Let us take, for example, a man with a bag of seed to plant. He scatters the seed all over the field. Each minute particle grows and bears fruit tenfold. He gathers the fruit and, after removing the seed, returns it to the bag, and now he has ten times as much as he had before. The simile is applicable to the unfoldment of man who, by passing through diversity, multiplies his acquirements and, finally, as the old soul, gathers the fruitage of his works and returns with them to unity. In place of the one latent possibility he originally brought with him, he carries back ten dynamic powers.

48. Realizing this fundamental unity of all form and all life manifesting through infinite

diversity, infinite time, and infinite space (as Herbert Spencer puts it), the student can understand the ancient occult demand for brotherhood. If all things are individualizing sparks from one neutral source, then each is a brother to everything else. Man is not to coalesce with but to cooperate with all living things. Upon the causal plane of life the principle of brotherhood is universal. Upon the form side alone is the primal One-ness diversified and the sense of unity lost. The unity buried in this diversity and hence unrecognizable by the young soul is seen in its true aspect as the sole Reality by him who has raised his spiritual consciousness above the plane of matter.

49. From the clash of material forms inevitably results the spark. When we raise our consciousness above the concrete, we see and realize the universal One-ness of life behind the illusional evil. This realization is one of the first steps on the path of wisdom. We are to include not only the human family but all Nature in our bond of brotherhood. It is our duty and responsibility to use every natural element constructively for the good of the Plan. If not, we overlook the bond of brotherhood which connects us with every part of the visible and invisible cosmos. All wanton destruction and carelessness respecting the rights of others generate inharmony in those who have failed

to recognize cooperation as the most fundamental and sacred of their spiritual obligations.

50. In the One-ness we find the ultimate of all manifestation. All diversity is destined to return again to its own source. Therefore it is said that the life of the great outpouring has its beginning and its end in its own center. All life is consequently symbolized by a great circle which returns again to that from which it came—a serpent with its tail in its mouth. This, however, can be understood in all its fullness only by those who have lived through the outpouring and found again the divine source.

The Mystery of the Number Two.

51. The number 2 is symbolic of the dual system of human thought, which views everything either from the standpoint of opposites or comparison. Things are judged in their relation to other things, but seldom, if ever, weighed and measured according to their own intrinsic merits. The mystic alone realizes that everything in Nature is a law unto itself and can be honestly evaluated when judged by its own standards alone.

52. The one outpouring reflecting itself in matter is called the *two*. This is the first negative number for when divided it leaves no remainder. All even numbers are called negative

and feminine, and are ruled by the moon. All odd numbers are called positive, because an odd number cannot be divided without leaving the First Cause, *One,* in the center. They are therefore under the dominion of the First Vibrant Power, the Sun.

53. As *One* is called the Number of the Father, so *Two* is the Number of the Earth— cosmic root substance or the base of form. This is the negative pole of life, called by ancients the Divine Mother in contrast to the vitalizing ray which carries the title of Great Father.

54. People who are mastered by bodies (which are the expressions of matter on the various planes of Nature) are referred to as negative. They may be courageous, violent, and apparently very positive, but in all things where the body rules the life they are negative. Hence, people who are ruled by appetites and passions, who are swayed by emotion and torn by things of the lower worlds, are said to be negative types, while those who rule their bodies in wisdom and integrity are called positive. All true mystics and occultists are positive.

55. When the vitalizing centers in the body are nourished by the spinal fires descending through the black serpent wound round the famous staff of Hermes man is said to be negative; while those who are raising these powers

[33]

and unfolding the cerebrospinal nervous system are said to be positive, for they are nourished by the ascending white serpent of wisdom raised by Moses in the wilderness.

56. As long as man is ruled by opposites, one of which is ever combatting the other, he is incapable of true spiritual growth. He must first unify these two opposing factors, which, like two thieves, steal his powers of concentration.

57. *Two* is said to be the number of unconsciousness, because the single spiritual power is broken or its flow impeded. It is also referred to as the number of contention, because the two extremes of Nature are always seeking mastery one over the other. Too often man fails to realize that domination on the part of either means the destruction of both; for in slaying its opposite it slays itself, since one pole cannot manifest without the other. Equilibrium is consequently the point of greatest efficiency in Nature.

58. When the center of consciousness is thrown out of its true position, it is rendered negative and impotent. Thousands of occult students are negative (and, consequently, incapable of growth) because they have allowed themselves to be led out of their own true center of consciousness. Some people wander millions of miles (figuratively speaking) from

their own centers of being and go off on endless tangents by following other people's advice. Both offender and offended lose sight of one of occultism's most important laws—namely, the necessity of unifying all opposites and synthesizing all philosophies.

59. Man's chief trouble is that when he weighs anything he also includes the human equation in one end or the other of the scale. Instead of weighing conditions as they actually are and remaining, as he should, at the point of equilibrium, his likes and dislikes distort his judgment, which, therefore, becomes null and void. Peace can never result from the rulership of extremes; for as the pendulum swings in one direction, so it will swing back and react in the opposite direction.

60. An excellent example of this is to be found in the political conditions of our day. For many hundreds of years—in fact, thousands—the world has been ruled by a patriarchy. Now the general trend is towards a matriarchy. An Amazonian form of government may appear at almost any moment. Many people believe this to be the true solution of the problem of life. The occult student, however, with his broader vision, realizes that this is merely shifting the weight of rulership from one end of the scales to the other and, consequently, can never bring about the

[35]

desired effect—namely, balance. The superiority of either extreme destroys the harmony of the Divine Plan. Only when these extremes are blended—at least, to the stage of constructive co-adunation—will religion, philosophy or politics ever find an answer to their eternal problems. Since earliest history, first one end has been up and then the other, and humanity must suffer from this condition until it learns that the greatest good is wrought when all things work together.

61. The number 2 is symbolic of discrimination; for it is the number of man's free will, which at this stage of his growth is not free but is merely the power of choice. Through experience with the opposites in Nature, man is developing the power of discrimination and by its application will remove much of his present suffering.

62. Those who would learn the mystery of the number 2 must learn how to use the power of thought to blend the opposites in Nature, for the mind is the uniting link between God and man. Without thought, man is an animal carried away by the sway of emotions. Those who do not think are *ipso facto* not human. Those who are unable to discriminate between what is better and what is best— maintain perfect balance as they walk between

the pillars of opposites—are not thinkers in the highest sense of the word.

63. Man will learn how to choose in but one way—through knowledge of the two extremes. Swinging like a pendulum, the Ego alternates both viewpoint and body from one life to another. Through this knowledge of opposites it gains the power of discrimination and finally learns how to blend differences that weaken into unities that strengthen.

64. Safe and intelligent judgment on any question depends upon the knowledge of the opposite phase of the thing discussed. Judgment of an individual does not depend solely upon his good points or upon his bad points, but upon a blending of the two. If you are giving a learned discussion on the subject of *Up,* be certain that you have considered equally the problem of *Down.* People whose knowledge is limited to only one side of a question are unfitted to pass judgment on any phase of it. This is a rule very frequently broken in Nature, for the majority of people who talk with glibness concerning things have totally ignored other viewponts which may have an important bearing upon the subject.

65. Every element in Nature has its opposite. In most cases the opposite of a thing is the lack of that thing. Light is an element; darkness is the absence of it. Knowledge is an

evolved state; ignorance is the lack of it. Good is a quality; evil is the least degree of good. As we evolve, we form a triangle out of the opposites by lifting our own center of consciousness above the plane in which lie the two points of our horizon.

The Mystery of the Number Three.

66. The number 3 is symbolized by the triangle, for it is the number of outpourings which radiated from divine Being in the process of creation. Its basic principles are spirit, soul, and body. This trinity manifests in the world of form as thought, desire, and action, which are the concrete attributes of the threefold divinity. These three principles or forces mold the destiny of all living things. The three spiritual phases are the centers of life and consciousness, while the three bodies (or methods of expression) are media by which the spiritual consciousness of man expresses itself in the objective world.

67. *Three* is also the number of the blended opposites for out of the duality of the *Two* there is born a child partaking of the natures of both of its progenitors but being a manifestation of neither in full. This divine *Three* is born in man as a result of the power of discrimination and the union of spirit, mind, and body. The secret formulae for this accom-

plishment has come down to us in the secret of the Philosopher's Stone, composed of its three elements—salt, sulphur, and mercury. The triangle is the simplest of geometric forms, in fact it might almost be called a geometric unit. And such it is in the world; for as father, mother, child, it is the fundamental cornerstone of all expression, generation, and regeneration in Nature.

68. The number *Three* is also known as the threefold path, for it symbolizes the highest expression of the three major divisions of human character. These three paths are symbolized by a philosopher, a priest, and a soldier. Occultism is the path of the philosopher, mysticism is the path of the priest, while service is the path of the soldier. All life seeking union with its source is advancing toward mastery along one of these three great rays.

69. The *Three* is also the number of the three worlds which the true Qabbalist is investigating with his self-evolved powers. It stands for the triple crown of the ancient Magus, who was king of heaven, earth, and hell; and, of course, it represents the three grand centers in the human body—the brain, the heart, and the generative system. The triple scepters of the Egyptian kings, the triple tiara of the Dalai Lama of Tibet, the three domed roofs of the Temple of Heaven at Pe-

king, all carry the same symbolism. Only when these three great universal natures are blended in harmonious understanding—each serving the other and the three uniting to serve the Divine—do we have the eternal triangle in man, which is symbolic both of his divine search and its consummation. Jakob Boehme, the great German mystic, said that these three natures were three witnesses by which God was known to men.

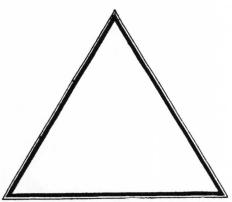

70. The number *Three* is symbolic also of balance or equilibrium; for the triangle is equilateral, meaning that all of its sides are of equal length. With its point upward it represents human aspiration and consciousness rising out of form to union with its divine source; with its point downward, it represents the triune powers descending into matter to mold it into a semblance of the trinity of spirit.

The Mystery of the Number Four.

71. *Four* is the symbol universally accepted to represent the path of accomplishment and the labors to be done; for, being the number of form and hence of earthly things, it is represented as a cube or stone within which life is imprisoned. Wherever this is found, it means that the labor of liberating life is the next thing to be accomplished. During involution man assumed bodies; now, since the point has turned and evolution is under way, man must concentrate his energies upon the labor of liberating life from its vestments of ignorance.

72. *Four* is the number of matter, because for our particular day of manifestation matter manifests as earth, water, fire, and air—action, vitalization, emotion, and thought. Science recognizes four basic principles as the key to all form, which is built up of their compounds. These four elements are carbon, hydrogen, nitrogen, and oxygen. The higher the plane of evolution, the more the life controls its own bodies. These four principles, however, form the *cross* upon which is crucified the spirit of life. *Four* is called the symbol of crystallization, and is also known as the number of impediment.

73. In astrology (a science well understood by the Qabbalists) *Four* is symbolized as a

[41]

square, one of the so-called evil aspects of a horoscope. It merely means that the points where the square falls, crystallization has not yet given place to vitalization. The square presents us with a problem to be solved, and is therefore a great benefactor in spite of its oppression. Matter is always opposing its own

vitalization because of its negation. Matter, symbolized by the cube block of salt in alchemy, is symbolic of the body, which, while unregenerated, seeks to smother and destroy the life imprisoned within. The square, therefore, is the symbol of the tomb, and this holy sepulcher is the tomb of matter in which our own spiritual nature lies buried. This is the cross of four arms which man must carry if he is to reach the footstool of Divinity. When our physical body is not properly taken care of, one corner of the square strikes us; when our emotions are not mastered, then the second corner of the square falls; when our vital systems are depleted, the third angle, as body crystallization, steps in; while our destructive thoughts react upon us as the fourth corner. When we have not been true to any of these, our nature collapses and we are buried in the tomb of matter under the symbol of the *Four*.

74. By his thoughts, feelings, and actions, man slowly transmutes this square tomb of stone into a cube of glass from which the light of spirit shines forth as through a protecting lantern. His present duty is to cleanse the glass; for though we see now through a glass but darkly, some time we shall know face to face. *Four* represents the number of bodies and the work we must accomplish with them. They are useful servants, but hard taskmasters.

The Mystery of the Number Five.

75. *Five* is the hand of the philosopher. It is made up of the four elements plus spirit, which—like the coordination between the human thumb and the fingers—cooperates with the four elements but is not with them for it works by opposition. *Five* is called the Christ, and in the *Tarot* it is the hierophant or priest, because it is the spirit of man rising from the

[43]

tomb of matter. Those who have lived through the laws of the *Four* and have mastered themselves have become the *Five*—i. e. liberated from the casket of matter. The geometric form of the condition is the pyramid, in which one corner rises from the four corners of the base. When the four elements have become the pedestal upon which the spirit stands as a city upon a hill and not with stone walls which close it in, then man has reached the spiritual number of the Five.

76. Man's development is the harmonizing of his centers of consciousness with the external planes in the universe by attuning the lesser self with the greater self. The tiny spark thus gains the ability to speak to its parent—the great spark. All this comes when the life is

freed from the form—not by destruction of form but by regeneration of the bodies, a process symbolized mathematically by the freeing of the *One* from the *Four*.

77. If our minds are befuddled or unbalanced, we cannot comprehend the mysteries of God. If our hearts are filled with misgivings or passions, we cannot have the divine compassion of the Christ. If we have expended our vital energy and wasted our substance in riotous living, we cannot attune ourselves to the living planes of the eternal. If our bodies are crystallized and broken, we cannot perform the daily labors that give us a right to our position in the Great Plan. These four bodies are our cross, upon which the *One* is crucified. Buried in materiality, we see only the *Four*. As we revivify and harmonize this cross through right living, then the *One* shines out and man becomes the divine *Five*.

78. When the *One* dictates to the *Four,* fear, selfishness, and egotism disappear. In their place is one who is great because of utter simplicity, great with the faith of a child and the wisdom of a god. Then the spiritual man, the *One,* is robed in the purified garments of the *Four*. But this great mystery—like all other true mysteries of the Qabbalah—must be lived before it can be understood. The fact that his name or birth path may be similar to any of

[45]

these numbers means nothing to the true Qabbalist. His conscious understanding as the result of having experienced these truths means all. Only those who have lived life through and have risen above life and its uncertainties can truly comprehend the mystery of the number *Five*.

The Mystery of the Number Six.

79. The first consideration in the study of the number *Six* is the well-known six-pointed star, or the two interlaced triangles commonly known as the Shield of David. Man consists of two interlaced triangles—the threefold spiritual body and the threefold form. They are his life principles and the casings of matter which are ensouled by them. In the trinity of creation are the three builders of the Temple who sit in council in the secret room. These three form the first triangle, with its point descending into matter. The three master-builders; the three lords of creation; the Brahma, Vishnu, and Shiva of India; the Father, Son and Holy Ghost of Christianity; the Ammon, Ra, and Osiris of Egypt—each of these groups represents the divine triangle. The ancient Qabbalists knew them as the vehicles of causation.

80. These three never manifest except through vehicles of expression. Therefore, in

order that they might make themselves known on this plane, it was necessary for the three kings to build a threefold body. This they accomplished and then took up their dwelling places in the brain, heart and generative system, which in man are their thrones.

81. *Six* is sometimes called the number of materiality, for it is symbolic of the union of spirit and matter. It really becomes a second symbol of equilibrium and is sometimes referred to as the soul. Man at the present time is symbolic of the union of spirit and matter, for he has barely passed the turning point where the higher begins to control the lower. This *Six* forms the protection or vehicle for the manifestation of the unknowable in man. The two triangles are symbolic of fire and water, and when these are interlaced they are said to stand for the Philosopher's Diamond. They also stand for the interblending of all pairs of opposites within man's own being.

82. *Six* also represents the six senses, the sixth sense being clear vision and the ability to function on the plane of the astral world, which is the next of our many latent faculties to be unfolded. This sense will have much to do in assisting man to gain mastery over his emotional nature.

83. The figure 6 is a line descending into a circle. The coil with the line descending is

[47]

symbolic of the serpent's coil, which descends in 9 and ascends in 6. Therefore, in the case

of *Six,* the serpent is returning upward to the power which was its source.

The Mystery of the Number Seven.

84. *Seven,* the immortal number of the Mosaic law, is called the day of completion; for it is said by the ancients that all things were made in seven days. This is true when understood from the esoteric standpoint. All life is divided into seven parts, and the passage of consciousness through these seven divisions constitutes what are known as the "days" of creation.

85. These seven parts are the centers of consciousnes—vowels, notes, colors, and senses in

[48]

the body of the man cosmic. The pathway of human evolution winds in serpentine fashion in and out through these seven centers, finally uniting them as beads upon its gleaming, golden thread.

86. The so-called seven days of creation are not numbered or divided by man made time. They are steps in the unfolding of the soul, and man finishes a day of creation when he bridges a certain gap between incidents and raises his consciousness one full rate of vibration over his former position.

87. The time may be seven minutes or seven million years, but regardless of how long it takes in these figures, man can never spend more spiritual time in his evolution than the seven creative days.

88. The seven centers within man's own being and the seven senses he is slowly evolving through contact with natural conditions show, when completed, that the soul has finished its days of wandering and is to be liberated upon the seventh day to start its own creative labors.

89. Seven fundamental laws mold all created things. No individual can be greater than these laws, and those who are greater than law among the spiritual hierarchies are far too great to doubt its powers. Every living thing has become subservient to certain laws as the

result of its gradual growth, and while the law never varies in its fundamental principles, its effects vary according to the combinations of intelligence upon which the law reacts. It is absolutely true that one man's meat is his brother's poison—not that the law changes, but its effects are different when striking variously attuned receiving systems.

90. One individual may live to be a hundred and nine on limeade and cottage cheese, while another could not live a week on such a diet. One individual may fall from an upper window and be only slightly bruised, while another slipping on the sidewalk is killed. One person may go to sleep on board a battleship while broadsides are being fired, while another is kept awake by the ticking of a clock. One is exposed for years to every variety of weather a rigorous climate can offer, and lives to be a hundred; another stands in a draft for a few moments and contracts a fatal case of pneumonia. Accordingly, all students, when advising others, should realize that their great work is to analyze reasons, to understand causes, and, most of all, to discover their own weak points and strengthen them as rapidly as possible.

91. It takes a person exceedingly wise to live his own life—realizing the way he is constituted, to act in harmony with the influxes of the law that affect him. While all students of

spiritual philosophy must realize the necessity of living a clean, wholesome life, they must give to all others that same freedom of expression which they wish others to grant for their own idiosyncrasies.

92. Cranks can never learn the mysteries of creation; for they have narrowed themselves to the circle of their own ideas, and no one who is narrow can ever know God who is broad. When we are inclined to be offended by a brother's act and concur in his damnation, we have the privilege of reminding him of his error—rather, what we believe to be his error. If he resents our interest, our responsibility ends. If we would know God, we must be God-like; and God will allow the drinker to drink and the raver to rave until the individual himself learns his lessons in his own way. In the vernacular of the street, God "butts" into no one's affairs; neither do God-like people.

93. *Seven* is the number of knowledge, and those who believe they are going to attain mastership in ignorance show that they are too ignorant to know what mastership is and, consequently, are incapable of applying a Master's power. None has ever gone to heaven who was not master of the seven liberal arts and sciences and all the various elements that make up the knowledge of the earth.

94. Man must realize that his first step is to

[51]

learn the laws of being. The second and more important step is that having found the laws of being in his own way, he must live them in his own way but always to the best of his ability.

95. To work out a problem and get it wrong often contributes more to the growth of the soul than to have someone else tell you and get it right. The student is always seeking for first-hand knowledge. He will not be satisfied with anything but the best; he desires to stand alone, and not to lean. The one who sits down and reasons it out gets a great deal more benefit than the one who asks questions and has them answered. Only the thinker and the worker learn the sacred mystery of the Qabbalah.

96. The *seventh day* is called the day of rest, and the whole religious world has argued and waxed eloquent and even wroth in its efforts to settle the moot point of which day is the seventh. Which day are we supposed to keep sacred? (We can't afford to keep them all!) Once again the true mystic sits back and would smile if he did not weep first. When we want to know what day is sacred to the worship of our God and Creator, let us no longer study a single creed but all religions, and then we find a singular thing. Each day of the week is sacred to some one of the great

religions, and on each one of the days of the week a great multitude of people meet and carry on their adorations. Man in his seven-fold nature must worship his God in thought, action, and desire seven days a week.

97. *Seven* is called the number of divine harmony, for it is the music of the spheres. All Nature is one great, harmonious melody to those who have harmonized themselves with it. Man must learn to recognize this eternal harmony and realize that all so-called inharmony is the result of inharmonious adjustments with himself within and his neighbor without. When we do not like something, let us like the result of that thing. If we do not like misery, let us learn to like the deepness and the understanding that comes out of it. If we do not like sickness, let us like the lesson that it teaches us. When we harmonize ourselves with the Plan, the mystic melodies of the seven spheres are echoed in our own seven-pillared temple.

The Mystery of the Number Eight.

98. *Eight* is the divine symbol of vitality. It is the symbol of the mystic marriage and of spiritual and physical regeneration. It is the great current without an end passing up and down through man as a golden band of light. *Eight* is the strange symbol inscribed by Na-

[53]

ture upon the puffed head of the Indian cobra, the symbol of the Logos, and the symbol of the universal creative power. All things in the universe are said to have come into being as a result of the twisting or spinning power of the figure 8.

99. *Eight* is considered by many as an unlucky number, another instance of sublime ignorance. The world is filled with people who have unlucky things and are troubled with unlucky days, astrological complexes, *et cetera*. Really they should not complain. It is the one who has to suffer as a result of their bad-luck attitudes that really is unfortunate. The bad luck of the universe is the misfortune of having people in it who are subject to misfortune.

100. There are no such things as bad numbers, bad rays, bad planets, unlucky birth hours, or similar afflictions; and those who are failures because of them would have been failures with anything else. All so-called misfortune is referable to the fact that at various times in the evolution of all creatures it becomes necessary for them to attune themselves with new cosmic influences. With those with which they have already become familiar they no longer have any trouble. In this world that which is easy has the preference and is called good, while that which opposes us because of

our own ignorance of it and which therefore requires effort to overcome, we call unlucky or evil. People with unlucky birth hours are merely confiding to their friends the fact that they are lazy—too lazy to exert themselves sufficiently to make those adjustments which they came into the world to complete.

101. The *Eight* stands for recompense—for the bringing back again of that which is lost. It is the return of those forces which have been redeemed from the animal world. It is the fusing or joining of the broken ends of the spiritual circuits which, combining in the body of man, form the spiritual wedding ring which unites the masculine and feminine natures within himself. Those who have not raised the sleeping serpent nor labored for years for the Hermetic Marriage and the Qabbalistic union can never understand the mystery of the number 8 until they, too, have wandered through its twisting coiling form.

The Mystery of the Number Nine.

102. *Nine* is called the number of humanity, or the symbol of incompletion. It is the number of man's bodies, for it takes nine months to build the human form. In China a child is a year old three months after birth, for the Chinese are a Qabbalistic nation. *Nine* is called by the ancients the broken wheel. There

are four seasons of three months each, spring, summer, autumn and winter. The winter months are the three yet unfinished in evolution; for which cause the Sun Spirit still descends into the earth on the 25th day of December and ascends at Easter, after spending his three days (months) in the tomb. This mystery is the story of Jonah's whale, which swallowed him and then cast him upon the shore.

103. Man is *Twelve* and so symbolized in nearly all of the ancient teachings, and *Twelve* is *Nine* plus *Three*. It is at this point that Freemasonry enters the scene, for the three steps of the Entered Apprentice, the Fellow-Craftsman and the Master Mason add to the nine months of physical birth the three degrees of spiritual birth, completing the broken wheel and making man the perfect *Twelve*.

104. Man must wander in the lower worlds until he makes of his *Nine* a *Twelve*, for there is happiness only in completion, and *Nine* is evil, so-called, only because it is unfinished; but man completes his birth when he goes up the three steps that lead to the Temple. (Occult legend states that some time in the future man will spend twelve months instead of nine as an embryo.) Three times three is *Nine*, and the thirty-three degrees of the Ancient Rite are very closely connected with the history of

man. As applicable to spiritual growth, each vertebra of the human spine represents a year, or a degree. As there are thirty-three segments in the human spine, we discover why there are thirty-three degrees in Freemasonry and why Jesus died in his thirty-third year and ascended to heaven. The human spine is the Jacob's Ladder of the ancients, upon which the angels ascended and descended. To the Qabbalist, the mystery of numbers is unveiled, for 666—the number of the Beast in Revelation—when its digits are added together makes eighteen, and eight and one equal nine; therefore man himself is the Beast. In the same document we understand that 144,000 shall be saved. When the digits of this number are added, the total likewise is nine, which proves that man also is to be saved as a unit or mass. Further applications of the system will occur to the student as he continues his research.

THE POWER OF INVOCATION AND
THE SCIENCE OF THE SACRED NAMES

PART III

105. The power of invocation, so-called, as used by the ancient Jews, has a wonderful spiritual meaning unsuspected by the average student of the magical arts. It was stated by the ancient rabbis that all the celestial influxes and personified natural forces had names, and these names and certain magic formulae were secretly communicated to those who had prepared themselves to receive them. This is practically all that the world knows concerning the secret instructions and strange conjurations used in the mystery of spirit invocation.

106. It was maintained by the ancient Masters of ceremonial magic and Qabbalistic arts that when the names of these great beings were properly invoked, the intelligence to whom the name belonged was forced to appear in answer to the summons of the magician. There were, however, certain instructions which must be carefully followed or serious harm would come to the magician. The disciples were instructed how they should build their circles, placing in them the various arti-

cles and implements which were prepared for the purpose. The magicians must have their censers and specially prepared incense, their swords, their rods strangely engraved with hieroglyphic figures, and their virgin parchments inscribed with seals and pentacles. If all these things were as they should be and the magician had inscribed the sacred name of the intelligence he wished to invoke, it would appear to him, usually with considerable attendant noise and tumult. The spirit would then await the instructions of the adept, for it was claimed by these magicians that they could control the intelligences belonging to the spiritual worlds of Nature.

107. Varying combinations of vitalizing rays, which we call the letters of the Hebrew alphabet, and the vowels which form the life of the alphabet were used to produce the conjurations of the ancient magicians. These men by their magic power had learned how to combine these symbols into the forms of great celestial beings, like Faust in his laboratory invoking the earth-spirit. Certain combinations of these vital energies inscribed on the virgin parchment of a purified body united the consciousness of the individual with the plane of Nature which he had invoked by the organic quality of his own life.

108. Man must learn that he is identical with

these letters. Every one of his thoughts is a letter; every action is a word; every combination of thought action, and desire, every combination of the four elements of his life, produces a name as he lives them. That name is the name of one of the lower planes of Nature; and every action attunes him to an external influx, which has been personified under the name of the angels.

109. *We are the living invocation, and our every thought and action spells out a word. These words are the names of things, and when we spell out their names they come to us.*

110. The combination of the consonants and vowels in the human body into words—the combinations of all the mental, emotional, spiritual, vital, and physical elements in man, which are the result of a sounding of these keynotes—brings an influx equal to the combination which man sends out. In invoking, the ancient Jew with his silver key used his letters. The modern mystic with his golden key uses his life.

111. Christianity, as found in the New Testament, is a mystic ritual to be unlocked only by the golden key of the Christian Qabbalah, which key is the vitalizing ray of the sun with its spiritual, mental, and physical regenerative powers. The key of the ancient Qabbalah was

the silver key of the moon, with its body and form-building propensities.

112. Christianity can never be understood until its students discover the sacred keys now hidden deep beneath its rubbish literal and physical. The reason the average interpretation of Christianity does not appease the soul hunger of the Christian student is because he has only the crystallized, external ritual. Its sublime magic—the magic of invocation, not as taught by the black magicians but as shown by the great adepts of the White School—is missing. There are two schools of Christianity. The physical, literal school would have died ages ago had it not been for the binding ties and the divine sacrifice of the spiritual school.

113. Each great religion has its sacred names symbolic of the state of development of those souls who are passing through it. The vowels and consonants composing these names in each case tended, when properly applied, to unite the seeker with his ideals. As Christian mystics (and this applies to all peoples, regardless of their beliefs) let us consider the invocation of the Christ.

114. It is a fact well known to students that the true names of the Exalted Ones are unspoken and unknown. Christ, like Krishna and Buddha, is a complimentary title, and the true name of the Great One who labored through

[61]

and inspired mankind is unknown to the lay brother, and must always remain unknown while he searches for it on paper or by word of mouth; for it is a sacred word written in the divine alphabets, not in the language of men. This sacred name is the golden secret of the priest initiate, and *he had to be it before he found it.*

115. The pure transcendentalist, in invoking a great Intelligence, drew his circles with chalks and pigments, prepared his physical robes of linen, his symbols and insignia, totally unaware of the fact that he was as far from the truth as East is from West, having failed entirely to grasp the true interpretation of Qabbalistic magic. Let us now see how a true Magus of the White Brotherhood sought to invoke the great Christ Spirit.

116. The true Magus stood in the center of his circle, but the circle was the sphere of his experiences; for, like the magician of old, he knew that if he left that circle all would be lost. Any true student knows that when he leaves the center of his own being, he forfeits all right to celestial power; for the circle is his own aura, while the life within enthroned in its center is the master of all conditions. The true magician was robed in the white garments of a purified body, in the silence and stillness of a harmonious being. He carried

the living offerings of his daily labors, and there with the vowels and consonants of the celestial alphabet as his own being he blazed forth in the living name that invokes all things. And when that invocation was made and he had invoked the Christ by being like the Christ, then he was one with the Spirit of Light, for nothing could refuse his call. His path finished, his mastership at hand, he had become one with the Christ by the power of the living word written in the celestial language radiating from the centers of his own soul. He then stood a Master of the Qabbalistic arts.

117. Let us now consider the black magician, who sells his soul to the demon. He also builds his circle, formed of his evil thoughts and emotions, and there he invokes his spirits by speaking the Divine Name; but now he can draw only the powers of negation and the principles of evil, because his life has spoken the word and it must draw that which is like unto itself.

118. We cannot invoke the Great Ones by chanting songs, for the only music that they can hear is the song of the lives we live. Many are the intelligences and planes of Nature which we attract by the power of invocation during our wanderings in the lower worlds; but always, regardless of what they may appear

[63]

to be, they are drawn not by the things we say but by the things we do.

119. The Qabbalah is a science by which that sacred name is learned, and the secret of the Qabbalah is that your own life is the word; and, whatever that is, that will you invoke. Man is the living magician, juggling with the elements of Nature. He is the living ritual, the living secret, and the living magic of the Qabbalah.

Made in United States
Orlando, FL
10 June 2024

47697072R00040